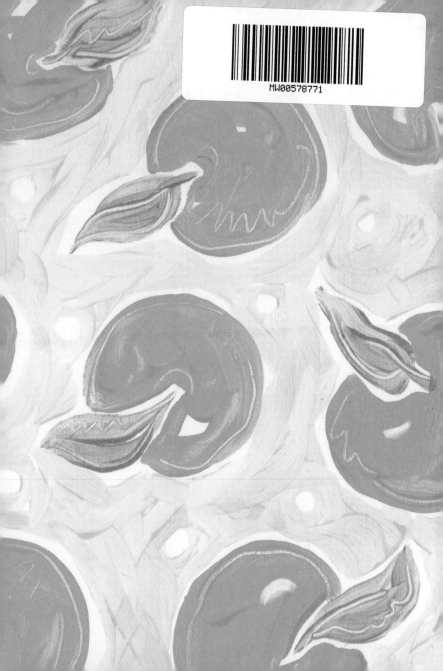

For:

_____

**You've been
a blessing to me!**

From:

_____

Teachers are a Gift from God
Copyright 2001 by Zondervan
ISBN 0-310-98654-0

All Scripture quotations, unless otherwise noted, are taken from the
Holy Bible: New International Version (North American Edition). Copyright 1973, 1978, 1984, by International Bible Society. Used by permission of
Zondervan Publishing House. All rights reserved.

The NIV and New International Version trademarks are registered in the United States Patent and Trademark Office by International Bible Society.

Requests for information should be addressed to:
Inspirio, the gift group of Zondervan
Grand Rapids, Michigan 49530
http://www.inspiriogifts.com

Project & Design Manager: Amy E. Langeler
Associate Editor: Molly Detweiler
Design: Kimberly Visser

Printed in China
02 03 04 /HK / 4 3 2

Teachers are a Gift from God

inspirio™

I feel the leap of excitement of a new school year, the anticipation of things yet to come. And beyond that, I feel that this is home, a place that tugs at my heart, a place where I belong. Above all, this is a place of love.

Help me to remember this moment, Lord, when my job seems overwhelming. Help me in those times to touch this moment of love, to find it when I need it most. Sustain me in your love, Lord, I pray.

PATRICIA ANN FISHER

4

The Sculptor

I took a piece of plastic clay
And idly fashioned it one day,
And as my fingers pressed it, still
It bent and yielded to my will.

I came again, when days were passed,
The bit of clay was hard at last.
The form I gave it, still it bore,
But I could change that form no more.

I took a piece of living clay
And gently formed it day by day
And molded with my power and art
A young child's soft and yielding heart.

I came again when years were gone,
It was a man I looked upon.
He still that early impress bore,
And I could change it, nevermore.

ANONYMOUS

Teaching takes time &

   energy, paying

attention to all the

Children,

helping them,

encouraging them,

reaching out to the quiet one, &

   Sometimes simply being there.

CAROLINE BLAUWKAMP

*W*herever they go, teachers always hear a little voice in their minds wondering, How can I use that in my class? They go to conferences looking for ideas and inspiration from other teachers. They watch television and movies and make little notes about ideas they see. One day Angela, a teacher friend of mine, and I were shopping at a garden center and she enlisted me, and two sales ladies, to try to catch a small lizard that was hiding in some plants. She wanted to take it back to school and surprise her fourth graders on Monday. (I drew the line at trapping it in my new purse.)

PAT MATUSZAK

A teacher effects eternity;
he can never tell where his influence stops.

HENRY B. ADAMS

∾

He who opens a school door, closes a prison.

VICTOR HUGO

∾

If you can read this, thank a teacher.

BUMPER STICKER

∾

Education is not the filling of a pail,
but the lighting of a fire.

WILLIAM BUTLER YEATS

That spirit of servanthood, which often is lacking in American culture, is much more visible among Africans—at least among African students at Moffat College of Bible in Kenya, where I have taught for several summers. Instead of the dog-eat-dog competition that is evident among my American students, I have noted a genuine concern for one another, especially in regard to grades at testing times. My African students appear most pleased, not when they alone perform well, but when the others perform well, also. Indeed, if they were all to receive As there would be jubilation. Not so with my American students, whose real satisfaction comes only from being on top.

I have had to do some soul-searching myself on this issue. The competition for grades and the struggle for recognition in athletics that characterized my own student days have been subtly replaced by other forms of competition that are more befitting teachers and writers. But such a spirit is not becoming for a follower of Jesus.

RUTH TUCKER

*T*here are two kinds of wisdom, the apostle James says: worldly wisdom that is contaminated, ambitious and envious; and heavenly wisdom that is pure, content, merciful and submissive. So to be spiritually wise a person must exhibit understanding, acceptance and peace.

The good life is peace—knowing that I was considerate instead of crabby, that I stood by faithfully when all the chips were down, that I showed impartiality when I really wanted my preference, that I was real in the midst of phonies, that I was forgiving.

LUCI SWINDOLL

Who is wise and understanding among you?
Let him show it by his good life,
by deeds done in the humility
that comes from wisdom.

JAMES 3:13

~

A wise mans heart guides his mouth,
and his lips promote instruction.

PROVERBS 16:23

~

Apply your heart to instruction
and your ears to words of knowledge.

PROVERBS 23:12

*T*he classroom was traumatic on my very first day in elementary school. Mother had packed my lunch and told me I was to eat it at recess. She did not say there would be two recesses! The first came at ten in the morning and lasted only ten minutes; by the time the bell rang for us to return to class, I had finished my lunch. The second, longer recess was the official lunchtime, and I had nothing to eat. I was mighty hungry by dismissal time at three o'clock and must have rushed out of the building. The principal did not like my haste and yanked my ear in reprimand.

DR. BILLY GRAHAM

12

Thank You, God, from a Teachers Heart

Thank you, God, for all the tasks that await me today
they tell me you have filled my life
with people who need me
and that you are planning to bless me
with new adventures.

Thank you, Lord,
for that stack of papers that need correcting
they give me something to work with
and show that my students are trying.
And I also thank you that I had to tell my class
to pick up their papers and pencils at the end of the day
in some places children have no paper
or pencils, but here we have extra.

PAT MATUSZAK

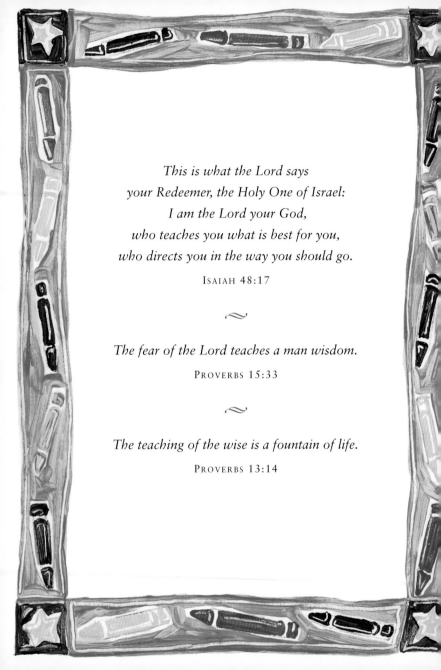

This is what the Lord says
your Redeemer, the Holy One of Israel:
I am the Lord your God,
who teaches you what is best for you,
who directs you in the way you should go.

ISAIAH 48:17

≈

The fear of the Lord teaches a man wisdom.

PROVERBS 15:33

≈

The teaching of the wise is a fountain of life.

PROVERBS 13:14

*I*n the ranks of music history, my seventh-grade music instructor will probably occupy the halls of obscurity, but in my memory he shines.

Mr. Strang wasn't a virtuoso clarinetist and I don't believe he even played the saxophone, the instrument I studied under him. He was a master, however, at the art of encouragement. I can still hear his voice after just about any of those long-ago, fumbling first lessons: Bob, great job.

As always, its been a pleasure. He really meant it. Amazing! You can pay for instruction. What you can't purchase is inspiration, and that is what my first music instructor gave me. He lit in me a spark that never went out, a love for music that's remained strong through the years. The first thing I learned from Richard Strang was the fingering for the note D. But his greatest, most enduring lesson has been the power of encouraging words to ignite vision and possibility, the best and the highest, within another person. Thank you, Mr. Strang!

BOB HARTIG

Ｈow important one life is. One
person can make such a difference. There
is something very powerful about having
someone believing in you, someone giving
you another chance.

SHEILA WALSH

≈

*Encourage one another and
build each other up.*

1 THESSALONIANS 5:11

Be kind and compassionate to one another,
forgiving each other, just as in Christ God forgave you.

EPHESIANS 4:32

≈

Do to others as you would have them do to you.

LUKE 6:31

≈

"Fix these words of mine in your hearts and minds,"
says the LORD, "tie them as symbols on your hands
and bind them on your foreheads.
Teach them to your children, talking about them
when you sit at home and when you walk along the road,
when you lie down and when you get up."

DEUTERONOMY 11:18–19

The assignment was to write about a positive experience. There was the usual grumbling, but Lucy, who had appeared to be asleep for three days, seemed genuinely interested, although from the looks of her first sentence she had forgotten the assigned topic. Oh well, I thought, at least she was writing. Later I read what she had written about a phone call telling her family that her brother was in prison: "The world went silent. Then it started to rain." Those two beautifully penned sentences were all I needed to remind me why I loved my thirty years in an English classroom.

DOROTHY CLORE

18

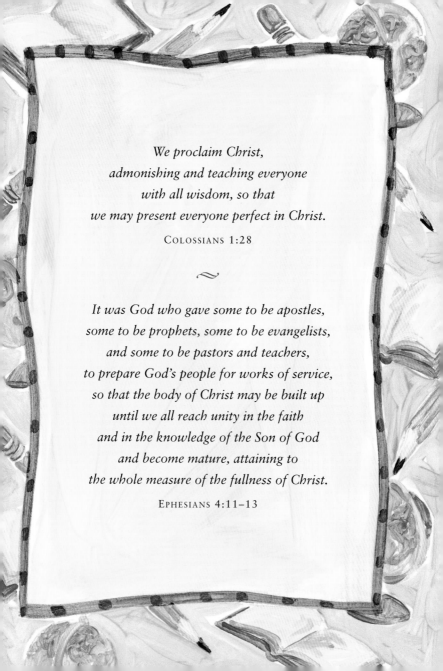

We proclaim Christ,
admonishing and teaching everyone
with all wisdom, so that
we may present everyone perfect in Christ.

COLOSSIANS 1:28

It was God who gave some to be apostles,
some to be prophets, some to be evangelists,
and some to be pastors and teachers,
to prepare God's people for works of service,
so that the body of Christ may be built up
until we all reach unity in the faith
and in the knowledge of the Son of God
and become mature, attaining to
the whole measure of the fullness of Christ.

EPHESIANS 4:11–13

The great Master said, "I see
No best in kind, but in degree;
I gave various gifts to each,
To charm, to strengthen, and to teach."

Henry Wadsworth Longfellow

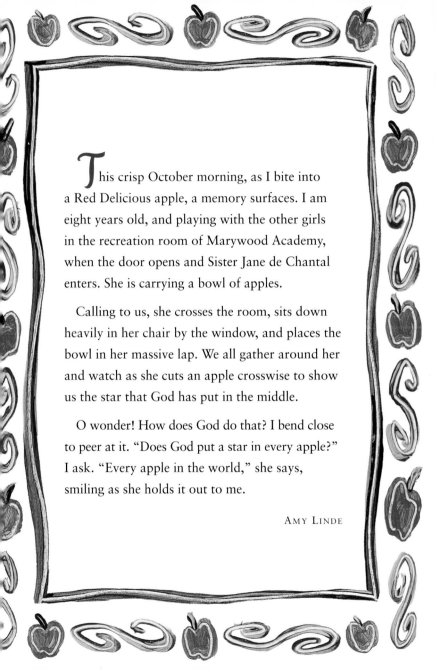

This crisp October morning, as I bite into a Red Delicious apple, a memory surfaces. I am eight years old, and playing with the other girls in the recreation room of Marywood Academy, when the door opens and Sister Jane de Chantal enters. She is carrying a bowl of apples.

Calling to us, she crosses the room, sits down heavily in her chair by the window, and places the bowl in her massive lap. We all gather around her and watch as she cuts an apple crosswise to show us the star that God has put in the middle.

O wonder! How does God do that? I bend close to peer at it. "Does God put a star in every apple?" I ask. "Every apple in the world," she says, smiling as she holds it out to me.

AMY LINDE

The greatest power of all is the power we have to invest ourselves in the lives of others. People need to see faith acted out before they are willing to hear the reason for it. Faith should be displayed in the world, not placed in a museum for theological tourists to admire. A hurting world needs what Christians have to offer.

CAL THOMAS

You will call,
and the LORD will answer;
you will cry for help,
and he will say: Here am I.....
If you spend yourselves in behalf of the hungry
and satisfy the needs of the oppressed,
then your light will rise in the darkness,
and your night will become like the noonday.
The LORD will guide you always;
he will satisfy your needs in a sun-scorched land
and will strengthen your frame.
You will be like a well-watered garden,
like a spring whose waters never fail.

ISAIAH 58:9–11

As teachers, we have a ministry and no time for less than the best. We have this ministry in the toughest of times. We have this ministry so we shall not lose heart. We have this ministry so we'll keep the faith and continue to pass it on, intact, to others. We have this ministry because we always expect the finest. We have this ministry so we always find time to share the Gospel. Even when we cannot speak the words, we know that our actions had better count because that's all there's going to be. We can proclaim the Word by who we are and what we do. It's not easy, but we can do it with the Lord's help.

PATRICIA ANN FISHER

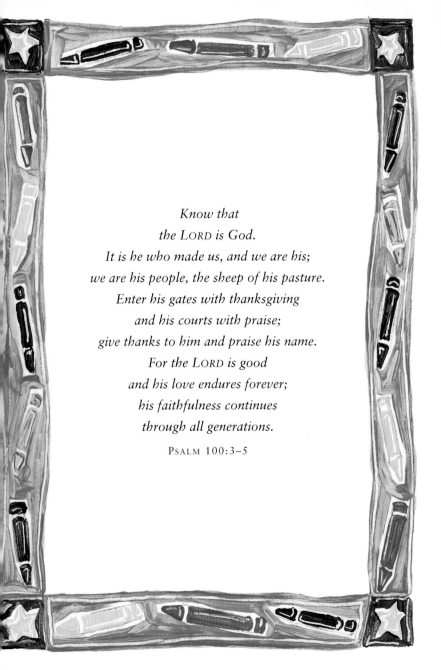

Know that
the LORD *is God.*
It is he who made us, and we are his;
we are his people, the sheep of his pasture.
Enter his gates with thanksgiving
and his courts with praise;
give thanks to him and praise his name.
For the LORD *is good*
and his love endures forever;
his faithfulness continues
through all generations.

PSALM 100:3–5

*a*s a baby, I had lost several fingers on my right hand through a severe car accident. The deformity never bothered me—and certainly never stopped me from getting my hands into everything—until I attended school. School kids taught me quickly the value of slipping my hand behind my back, keeping it in my pocket whenever possible, and stretching my sleeves so my hand could wriggle into a hiding place while still holding a book. I didn't care about not having fingers—I could still play the piano and ride my bike—but I did care about looking different.

One day, in grade three, my teacher came to my desk and whispered that the principal would like to see me in his office before I went out for recess that day. Now, I was scared of my principal. I sat in my desk seat staring at the clock, feeling suddenly very hot.

When recess came, I faced the inevitable. I said goodbye to my best friend, who promised to pray for me. I knocked on the door, expecting to see Mr. Kloster's stern eyes on the other side of the glass, staring into me.

Strangely, Mr. Kloster smiled and beckoned me in.

"Have a seat, Heather. I'm so glad you could come." I didn't reciprocate the feeling; instead, I looked at the floor.

"Heather, I know you've been attending this school for the last three years, but I hadn't noticed a certain something special about you until last week. And when I did, I realized that we have something in common."

I looked up at him and he held up a deformed hand. My eyes must have gone buggy because Mr. Kloster laughed. "You didn't notice it about me either, then, eh? I guess we're even." He had a nice laugh.

After that we told each other our stories, sharing some of the frustrations of our handicap. I soon forgot all about my best friend and stayed with Mr. Kloster the entire recess. It

was the bell that called our conversation to a close. As I was about to leave, Mr. Kloster said, "You're a beautiful young girl, Heather. I'm glad we have something in common."

I smiled and was glad too.

HEATHER GEMMEN

27

He who dwells
in the shelter of the Most High
will rest in the shadow of the Almighty.
I will say of the LORD,
"He is my refuge and my fortress,
my God, in whom I trust."

PSALM 91:1

∿

There is no way
I could be a teacher without constant prayer
and ongoing conversation with God.
Many other teachers
have told me that they feel the same.

PATRICIA ANN FISHER

The most important element for teachers is that you like children—because kids know when they are liked, and they know when they are not. The eyes of children see beyond masks and professional manners—they see the real you. Love your work. Cherish your sense of humor and enjoy the little ones entrusted to your care.

MRS. G

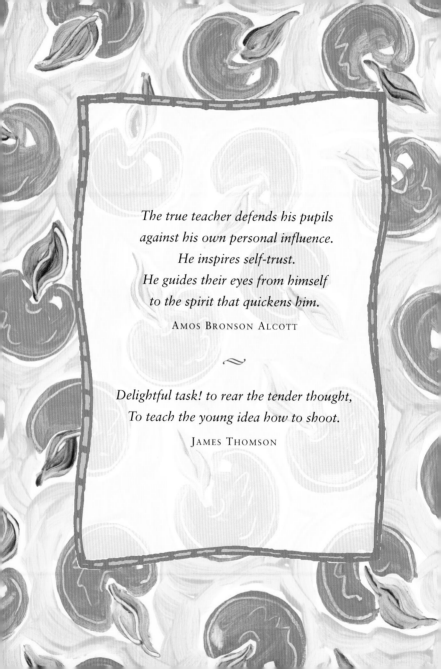

The true teacher defends his pupils
against his own personal influence.
He inspires self-trust.
He guides their eyes from himself
to the spirit that quickens him.

AMOS BRONSON ALCOTT

Delightful task! to rear the tender thought,
To teach the young idea how to shoot.

JAMES THOMSON

No matter what rosy picture the movies or books portray about teaching, we cannot reach every student. We may only see the results of our work years later, rather than before a semester ends. Once in a while a student realizes the help he or she was given in the classroom and calls or comes back to visit—those are the golden moments. But often the teacher never hears a thank you. We just have to have faith that the fledglings we fed, then pushed from the nest have gone on to safe havens with the skills we taught.

TOM

I took our fourth- and fifth-graders to the symphony today. It tickled me to look over and see two fourth grade boys with a copy of the instrument family color sheets that we completed in music class. They were diligently searching the orchestra for each instrument listed or illustrated on their page. It was very impressive that it was important enough to the boys to bring the sheets with them.

CHLOE, A FOURTH GRADE MUSIC TEACHER

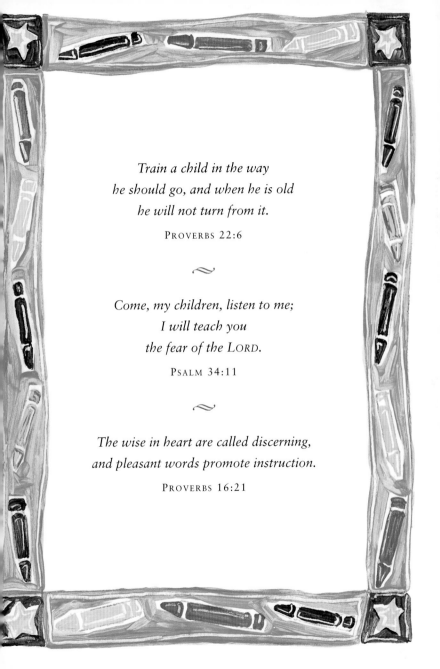

*Train a child in the way
he should go, and when he is old
he will not turn from it.*

PROVERBS 22:6

~

*Come, my children, listen to me;
I will teach you
the fear of the LORD.*

PSALM 34:11

~

*The wise in heart are called discerning,
and pleasant words promote instruction.*

PROVERBS 16:21

$\mathcal{O}$ne of the things that I have learned after being a home school mom for many years is that learning is not confined to the textbook. Some of our best "teachable moments" have occurred when doing an ordinary task which suddenly presents an incredible opportunity for an object lesson.

One such opportunity presented itself when my five-year-old daughter and I were outside doing some yard work. While I was pulling weeds, my daughter was busy filling a bucket with water, using the hose. After the bucket was full, she would dump it out in the driveway and start over.

After watching her do this three or four times, decided that it was time for a lesson in ecology and stewardship of the earth's resources. I proceeded to explain to her that dumping the water in the driveway was wasting it, and that if she wanted to have fun filling the bucket, she should use the water by dumping it in the garden or the flowerbed. She understood, and so ended the lesson—so I thought. That night as I was tucking her into bed she said, "Mom, if God doesn't use me before I die, will I be wasted?" Stunned by such a deep thought for such a little girl, I was momentarily without a response.

"Where did you hear that?" was all I could muster. "I just thought of it. You know how if you dump a bucket of water out without using it it's wasted?" she asked.

"Yes ..." I replied, beginning to see the direction she was coming from.

"Well, it's the same with people, you know? God made us, and someday we're going to die. And if God doesn't use me before I die will I be wasted?"

We went on to have the most precious talk about God's plan for her life, and how I was sure that God would use her! He already had! I was awestruck at how God had taken a simple lesson and turned it into a deep spiritual truth in a little girl's heart. We never know how God will use what we teach, and from that moment on I had a much deeper respect for the awesome privilege and responsibility that I held as the teacher of children.

LORI

35

The two people most needed in a school are the custodian and the secretary. I smile as I remember the wise advice of an education professor in college: "Be sure to get to know the custodian and the secretary at your school. They're the people who run the place." Liz, our school secretary, only works part-time because of the size of our school, but she always does a full-time job in the four hours she works.

PATRICIA ANN FISHER

O LORD, you have searched me
and you know me.
You know when I sit and when I rise;
you perceive my thoughts from afar.

PSALM 139:1–2

Let me understand
the teaching of your precepts;
then I will meditate
on your wonders, O LORD.

PSALM 119:27

The discerning heart seeks knowledge.

PROVERBS 15:14

The teacher I'll always remember was my senior high English teacher, Helen Fitting. She just loved reading and words. When she would read us a new selection, the expression on her face was as though she were tasting double-chocolate cheesecake! Then she'd just smile and look around the room for a few seconds and see if anyone else caught the experience. We very often did and developed a "taste" for literature. She taught us to love words.

PAT MATUSZAK

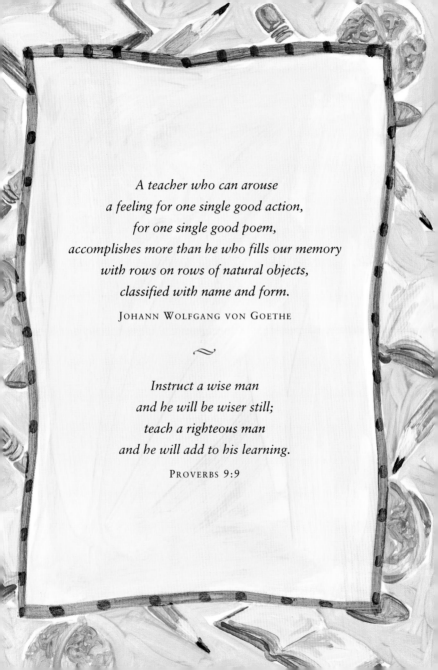

A teacher who can arouse
a feeling for one single good action,
for one single good poem,
accomplishes more than he who fills our memory
with rows on rows of natural objects,
classified with name and form.

JOHANN WOLFGANG VON GOETHE

Instruct a wise man
and he will be wiser still;
teach a righteous man
and he will add to his learning.

PROVERBS 9:9

No one has yet realized
the wealth of sympathy, the kindness
and generosity, hidden in the soul of a child.
The effort of every true education should be
to unlock that treasure.

EMMA GOLDMAN

~

Jesus said,
"Whoever humbles himself like this child
is the greatest in the kingdom of heaven.
And whoever welcomes
a little child like this in my name
welcomes me."

MATTHEW 18:4–5

$\int$ome excerpts from a paper written by a little girl about her teacher:

Mr. Alexander was my fifth-grade teacher. He was really nice. Mr. Alexander was tall, really smart, funny and nice.

His favorite subject was writing or language arts. He taught us how to use a writing pyramid. How to write detailed sentences.

Mr. Alexander had a fun way of teaching us different subjects. We usually played games that helped us. He also organized a chess club where anybody could sign up.

All the kids in my class are my friends. These are mostly all my friends because Mr. Alexander made us and then we began to like each other.

*a*t recess time the children head eagerly for the playground, except those who have asked all morning when recess is. Now they are the ones asking if they have to go out. I nod. "But it's cold," they protest. (Why didn't they think about that earlier when they were asking about recess every five minutes?) In any case, they lose.

The ten-cent cup of coffee in my friend's classroom has more appeal than a roomful of first-graders in desperate need of a break to get the wiggles out.

The day goes on. Juan forgot his lunch. Liza threatens that her grandmother will beat me up because I allowed her to get her new coat dirty. It becomes a day like any other.

Why does any intelligent person teach, I ask myself as I wearily usher the last of the thirty-two out of the room. Then Liza comes dashing back in. She had forgotten her coat, the dirty one. On her way out she yells, "Bye, Mrs. Fisher. I love you."

That's what's so wonderful about teaching—children don't hold grudges, not even for dirty coats.

PATRICIA ANN FISHER

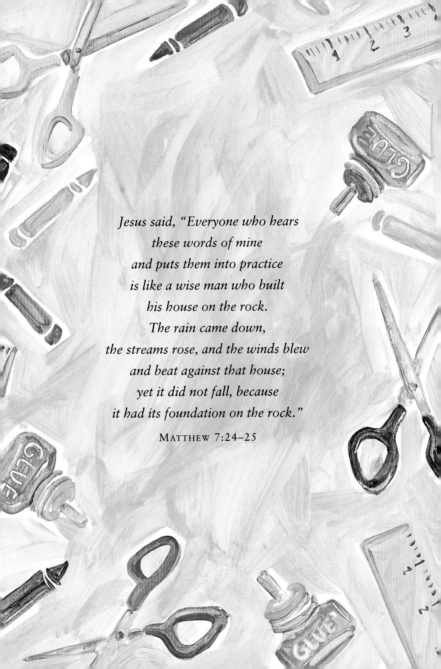

Jesus said, "Everyone who hears
these words of mine
and puts them into practice
is like a wise man who built
his house on the rock.
The rain came down,
the streams rose, and the winds blew
and beat against that house;
yet it did not fall, because
it had its foundation on the rock."

MATTHEW 7:24–25

*a*n assistant superintendent challenged our teaching staff to make a daily, positive phone call to parents. "It'll make a real difference in their lives, in your classroom, and in your career." It sounded like a nice idea, but it would also be one more thing to do in our already overbooked days. My dedication to the project lasted only a semester. Life got busier, no one was checking up on me, I slacked off, and the assistant superintendent moved on to another school district.

Years later, thinking that the promise of positive calls might cut down on discipline problems, I began asking students for their home phone numbers. Some put down pizza delivery numbers, but some write, "Please call!!!" next to their correct home numbers. Parents, after they quit holding their breath waiting for bad news, are grateful: "You've made my day!" or "This is certainly an unexpected surprise!"

I think often of my friend Mike Freeland, the assistant superintendent. He died suddenly several years ago, his life shortened, seemingly unfairly. Somehow I hope he knows that I've finally gotten around to making those phone calls. He was right; they make a great deal of difference.

DOROTHY CLORE

In everything set them an example
by doing what is good.
In your teaching show integrity,
seriousness and soundness of speech.

TITUS 2:7–8

≈

Jesus said, "Knock and the door
will be opened to you.
For everyone who asks receives;
he who seeks finds; and to him who knocks,
the door will be opened."

MATTHEW 7:7–8

≈

"I guide you in the way of wisdom
and lead you along straight paths,"
says the LORD.

PROVERBS 4:11

Some Letters from Kids:

Mr. Rozek:

Thank you for being a great teacher. You were very patient with me and I appreciate that. Thanks for everything.

FROM CHRISTINA

*B*efore I met Mr. Rozek I had a real tough time with teachers. I was always scared of them. But when I was a freshman and I had Mr. Rozek he changed everything for me. He made the class fun and interactive. He gave and we gave. He was personable. He made me glad to go to school! Before, I thought I was dumb. But Mr. Rozek made work fun! Believe it or not he made me love Shakespeare!

~

*F*rom Mr. Rozek I learned that teachers are people (so naturally I lost my fear). I also learned that I am not dumb.

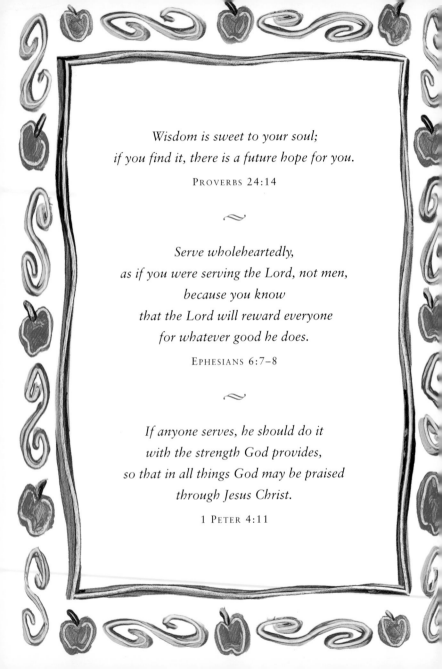

Wisdom is sweet to your soul;
if you find it, there is a future hope for you.

PROVERBS 24:14

Serve wholeheartedly,
as if you were serving the Lord, not men,
because you know
that the Lord will reward everyone
for whatever good he does.

EPHESIANS 6:7–8

If anyone serves, he should do it
with the strength God provides,
so that in all things God may be praised
through Jesus Christ.

1 PETER 4:11

$\mathcal{G}$od promises that the heart that seeks him sincerely will find him. He wants to prove to you that this promise is true. Let him. Whenever you sense a hunger in your soul, a desire left unquenched, a disappointment that defeats you, turn to him and ask him to fill your deepest needs in the appropriate way. Then look for your life to change. By transferring your ultimate dependence to God, you will gain assurance of his unfailing love, power to set boundaries, and power to hold others accountable. You will be able to face difficulties with confidence and fulfill the dreams God has in store for you.

CONNIE NEAL

*I*t seemed like a good idea at the time ...

The zoo in a nearby city offered to bring some of the smaller animals to visit each classroom. But then I found out what the zoo considers a small animal. Small is not a word I use to describe boa constrictors. The children and I watched in awe as the zoo volunteer described the boa and its habitat while allowing the snake to wind itself around her neck. I shudder.

"Now I'm going to let each of you pet Angelo," the volunteer announced. The girls in the class all gasped, and some of the boys' faces turned a little green. "And to prove there's nothing to fear, your teacher will go first."

Lord, is this absolutely necessary? Will these children be permanently damaged if their teacher refuses to touch a snake?

My heart began to thump, my hands became clammy, and my shadow ran from the room screaming. But the teacher in me smiled reassuringly at the thirty-two faces intently watching me. I took a deep breath and reached toward the snake. The boa felt warm and dry; it was my own hands that felt cold and clammy.

PATRICIA ANN FISHER

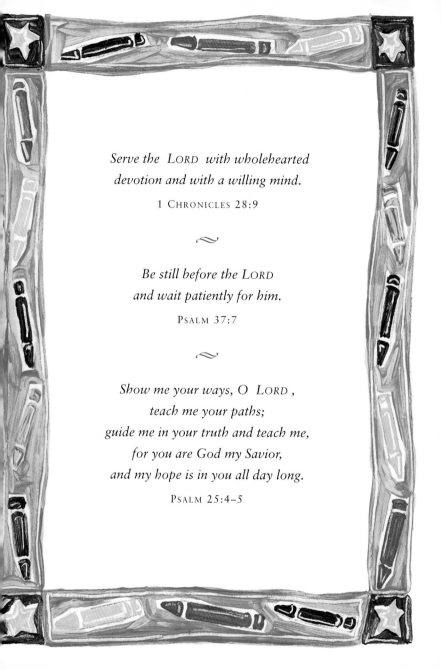

Serve the LORD *with wholehearted devotion and with a willing mind.*

1 CHRONICLES 28:9

∽

Be still before the LORD
and wait patiently for him.

PSALM 37:7

∽

Show me your ways, O LORD ,
teach me your paths;
guide me in your truth and teach me,
for you are God my Savior,
and my hope is in you all day long.

PSALM 25:4–5

Teach us, good Lord,
to serve Thee as Thou deservest:
To give and not to count the cost;
To fight and not to heed the wounds;
To toil and not to seek for rest;
To labor and not ask for any reward
Save that of knowing that
we do Thy will.

St. Ignatius of Loyola

One of the best examples of patient encouragement I ever witnessed was that of sixth-grade band director Jim Mollema. One day during the first weeks of school, I was passing the band room on the way to my classroom when I heard a screeching noise that sounded as if it could only have been made by the simultaneous violent deaths of dozens of unfortunate cats. Then the screeching stopped just as I passed the door.

Peeking in unobserved, I saw Jim standing at the director's podium with his baton lightly poised as he addressed a class of about fifty sixth-graders, proudly holding various band instruments in their laps.

"That was very nice," he said in his gentle, calm voice with genuine enthusiasm. One would have thought the aural assault the students had just produced was the sound he had been waiting to hear all his life. "Now let's go back to the top and try that again, shall we?" he smiled.

This man gained my undying respect as he repeated the same loving exercise every day for the whole year.

PAT MATUSZAK

In about 1930 [when about twelve years old], I gave my first speech. I portrayed Uncle Sam with a long beard and a tailcoat in a pageant at Woodlawn School. My mother was a nervous wreck after teaching me the speech and listening to me practice it until I knew it word perfect. My knees shook, my hands perspired, and I vowed to myself that I would never be a public speaker! But Mrs. Boylston, the principal of Woodlawn, told Mother I had a gift for it.

DR. BILLY GRAHAM

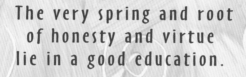

The very spring and root
of honesty and virtue
lie in a good education.

Does the place you're called to labor
Seem too small and little known?
It is great if God is in it,
And He'll not forget His own

Little is much when God is in it!
Labor not for wealth or fame.
There's a crown—and you can win it,
If you go in Jesus' Name.

KITTIE L. SUFFIELD

I don't like meetings of any kind, but Peggy, our principal, does. She has teachers' meetings every Tuesday after school. Consequently, every Tuesday I want to give up teaching altogether. Teachers' meetings held at the end of the day are the worst, because they can go on for hours. Peggy's always do.

If Peggy notices our dismay, she does not acknowledge it. Instead she begins to read the calendar of events. Her voice drones on, and the minutes crawl by. We all can read, and we all have our own copies. I begin to feel like a child being kept after school for some unknown offense. Bone-weary, I watch the clock approach 5:30. An army recruiter could enlist the entire faculty right now, I think to myself. We all would do nearly anything to escape.

Suddenly I feel a giggle. Oh no, not now. When extremely tired, I am given to uncontrolled bouts of giggling. "Go get a drink, Pat," Peggy sternly commands. I turn on the water fountain, forgetting for a moment that it is the one that shoots water across the room. I realize one second too late that the spray is aimed at Peggy. As water pours down Peggy's face, Shelly reaches for paper towels and I try unsuccessfully to get the faucet unstuck.

"I'm really sorry, Peggy," I try to apologize, but I am doubled over with laughter. Shelly sits at the table, tears of laughter rolling down her face. Marty, the kindergarten teacher, gets up to help but slips on the wet floor and lies sprawled facedown on the tile, laughing so hard she can't get up.

What should have been a five-minute cleanup job takes us fifteen because we spend most of the time in unrestrained laughter. In these unplanned, unprogrammable moments we find the togetherness Peggy demands of us.

PATRICIA ANN FISHER

Learning to Pack My Suitcase
with Help from Sister Jane

"Learning to pack my suitcase" was a weekly chore
    you set for me in boarding school each Thursday night
    before my weekends home.

Sitting beside you on the dorm's tile floor,
    I stacked my dresses, folded soiled shirts, and rolled my
    dirty socks, under your watchful eye.

"How stupid," I thought, seizing my cotton slip.
    Why fold my dirty underwear to take them home to mother?
But there you were, week after week,
    your black veil falling across your outstretched arm,
    as patiently you bent me to the task.
These long years later, planning for a trip, I think of you,
    dear sister.

Packing my suitcase is a habit now. The trip all planned,
    my choices made, I fold and stack without a second thought,
except the one I have of you this moment,
    bending to me, and slipping in among my schoolgirl's clothes,
    a teacher's gifts, invisible 'til now, for which
I never thanked you.

AMY LINDE

58

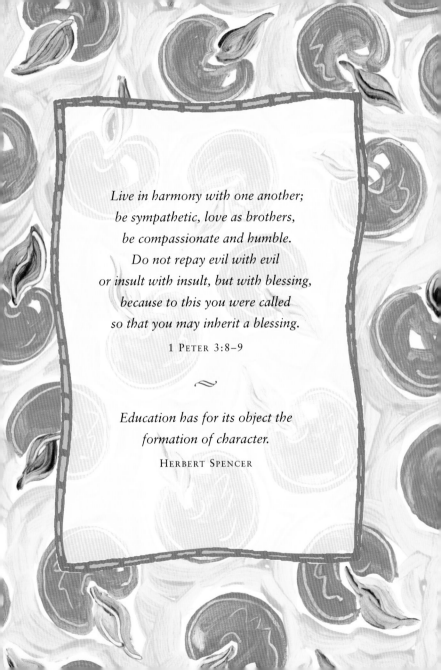

Live in harmony with one another;
be sympathetic, love as brothers,
be compassionate and humble.
Do not repay evil with evil
or insult with insult, but with blessing,
because to this you were called
so that you may inherit a blessing.

1 PETER 3:8–9

∾

Education has for its object the
formation of character.

HERBERT SPENCER

A student's letter:

The best teacher I have ever had—one who will live forever in my memory—is Mr. Rozek, my ninth-grade English teacher. During my freshman year in high school, he made it easier for me to cope with being a "little fish in a big pond."

He was comical, inquisitive, and fun-loving. He created activities that made learning enjoyable. He had an easygoing manner, but we learned a lot.

I remember once Mr. Rozek let two students from our class take a trip to the school store and purchase a vast amount of "goodies" because a lot of us were hungry. And then there were various jokes that made class time exciting to be a part of. He was the best!

In my opinion, the main quality which distinguishes Mr. Rozek from the rest of my high school teachers is that he often expressed how much he cared. When a student had excessive absences, he didn't make sarcastic remarks. He would simply say, "I wonder what's going on with him/her?" He never judged a book by its cover; he would always make his judgment by the content inside.

For me personally, Mr. Rozek brought new dimensions to the classroom and to my high school experience. He inspired me to think, to create, and to take pride in my work. These are habits that will last me a lifetime.

GERRY

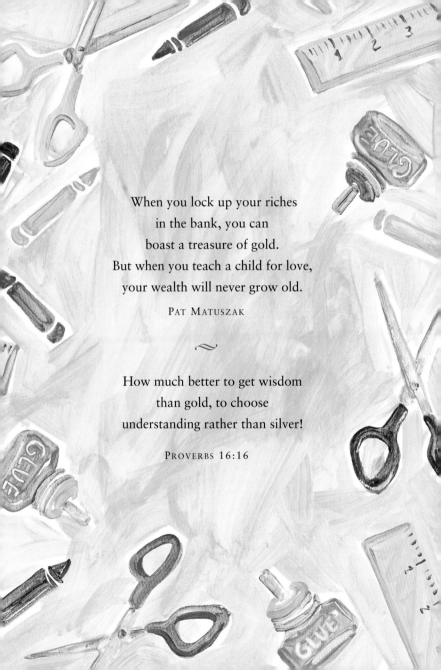

When you lock up your riches
in the bank, you can
boast a treasure of gold.
But when you teach a child for love,
your wealth will never grow old.

PAT MATUSZAK

How much better to get wisdom
than gold, to choose
understanding rather than silver!

PROVERBS 16:16

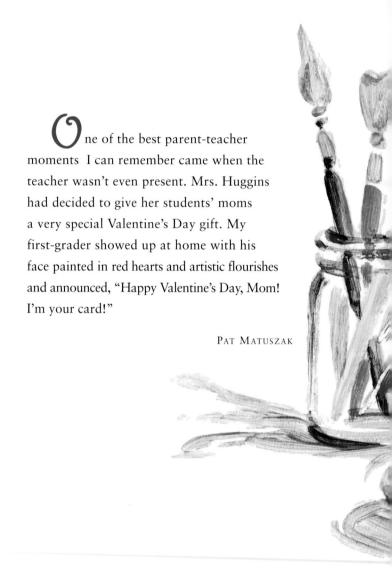

One of the best parent-teacher moments I can remember came when the teacher wasn't even present. Mrs. Huggins had decided to give her students' moms a very special Valentine's Day gift. My first-grader showed up at home with his face painted in red hearts and artistic flourishes and announced, "Happy Valentine's Day, Mom! I'm your card!"

PAT MATUSZAK

*M*y favorite teacher was Mr. Cheselka, who taught sixth grade at Hilton Elementary. He taught us more than academics—he told us stories about life. He would give us a history lesson, then apply it to everyday circumstances we could understand. He often used humorous examples and personal stories that made history come alive for people our age. We could tell he liked us and enjoyed what he was doing.

BRUCE BIGGINS

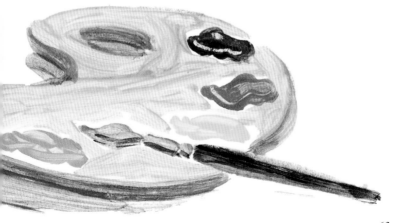

I was fortunate to have been able to study dance with Dorothy Lester when I was a teenager. She was a great influence in my life as a dancer and later as a dance instructor. There are a lot of good dancers in the world, but to be a good instructor, you have to have the gift to explain to someone how to pull the talent out of her inner self—describing a movement in a way that gives her the understanding of how it's supposed to feel to do it correctly. And you have to instill in her a respect for hard work. Whenever I felt like taking the day off of practice, I could hear my teacher's voice saying, "For every day you don't dance, it will take you two days to make it up."

ELISA DiSIMONE

My younger sister knew what I was going to major in at college before I ever told her. "Teaching, of course," she said. "You think I'd forget all those times when we were little and you made us play school so we could be your students?"

JANE TERRANOVA

~

To waken interest and kindle enthusiasm is the sure way to teach easily and successfully.

TRYON EDWARDS

*I*f you think driver's education teachers have a hazardous teaching assignment, consider this testimony from an Air Force jet pilot about his teacher:

Captain Steve Warrior (yes, it's his real name!) was a great instructor pilot. He made me simplify things. I had picked up so many pointers and techniques from other instructors and lectures that everything became confusing. But he would just give me a direction, then say, "Don't think about everyone's techniques— just make it happen." He'd save criticism for when we got on the ground, and just tried to make me enjoy the flight. When you are flying, the instructor is wearing a mask and you can't see his expressions—he looks and sounds like Darth Vader— but Captain Warrior always had a smile when he got out of the cockpit.

Lt. John Matuszak

I wish [my teacher] was smart enough to teach second grade, too, next year.

WILLIAM GOUMAS, FIRST-GRADE PUPIL

~

*A professor can never
better distinguish himself in his work
than by encouraging a clever pupil,
for the true discovers are among them,
as comets amongst the stars.*

CARL LINNAEUS

I stopped my car for a traffic light, and a little girl and her dad walked across the street in front of my car. She wore bright red overalls, and her black silky hair flowed down her back. Her small white sneakers kept pace with her father's strides. I smiled when I saw her tiny hand wrapped tightly around one of her father's fingers; I remembered doing the same with my father. In that moment, I longed to be a child again.

I drove on thinking about my current frenzy to get things done—a woman on the go but still God's child. A sense of safety, of well-being, of security came over me, and I wrapped my hand around God's finger.

KATHY TROCCOLI

I coached football for seventeen years and wrestling for twenty-three years. When I got out of coaching, one of the things that I missed the most was the time spent before the contest, preparing the boys for competition. I always included a verse of Scripture and a three-minute commentary. And I always closed in prayer. As the season progressed, the boys began to anticipate this portion of our preparation. The presence of the Holy Spirit in our locker room (or bus or corner of a hallway) powerfully affected our team, making us brothers in Christ.

JACK HUDSON

One of the funniest moments that happened to me as an elementary teacher was when I ran into several third-grade students at the local grocery store. They looked at me with disbelief for a moment; then one of them finally exclaimed, "Mrs. Matuszak! You buy groceries!" I guess they had never thought of a teacher having a life outside of the classroom.

PAT MATUSZAK

A builder built a temple
    He wrought with care and skill.
Pillars and joints and arches
    Were fashioned to meet his will;
And men said when they saw its beauty:
    "It shall never know decay.
Great is thy skill, O builder,
    Thy fame shall endure for thee."
A teacher built a temple;
    She wrought with skill and care,
Forming each pillar with patience,
    Laying each stone with prayer.
None saw the unceasing effort;
    None knew of the marvelous plan;
For the temple the teacher built
    Was unseen by the eyes of man.
Gone is the builder's temple;
    Crumbled into the dust,
Pillar and joint and arches
    Food for consuming rust;
But the temple the teacher built
    Shall endure while the ages roll;
For that beautiful, unseen temple
    Was a child's immortal soul.

AUTHOR UNKNOWN

Jesus said,
"Let the little children come to me,
and do not hinder them,
for the kingdom of God belongs to such as these.
I tell you the truth,
anyone who will not receive
the kingdom of God like a little child
will never enter it."
And he took the children in his arms,
put his hands on them
and blessed them.

MARK 10:14–16

*P*icture yourself in the time of Christ, the sun warm on your hair and your sandals dusty as you watch Jesus surrounded by numerous people. Hear the indignation in Jesus' voice when the disciples try to shield him. Hear the loving care and concern in his voice as he holds out his arms inviting the children to come.

The children love Jesus, and they touch him. One little girl lays her head on his shoulder. Jesus takes time for each one ... blessing, touching, loving, and sending each back to his or her parents with joy. Who can ever be the same after having been touched by Jesus!

Right now, be a child in the arms of Jesus, whatever your age. Let him hold you. We are all children who desire to rest in those strong arms. In reassuring words he speaks to you:

"My child, I care about you. I love you unconditionally. Trust me. I love you."

ROSALIND RINKER

God is calling each of us to a life of adventure. Remember, an adventure is not an adventure unless there is some risk involved. Are we willing to take risks in our walk with Jesus? Are we willing to look a little foolish from time to time as we seek to develop new talents? If we are, God will continue to bring us new opportunities of service. The joyful reward is this: One day we will stand before our great God and hear him say, "Well done, good and faithful servant!" (Matthew 25:21).

HOPE MACDONALD

$\mathcal{O}$nce I asked my brother Chuck if he'd rather have wisdom or youth, presupposing the two don't reside in the same person at the same time. Without hesitation he answered, "Oh, wisdom, Sis, hands down. That way I don't keep doing the same dumb things I did as a kid." Then with a twinkle in his eye he added, "Of course I'd really prefer having wisdom in a young body."

LUCI SWINDOLL

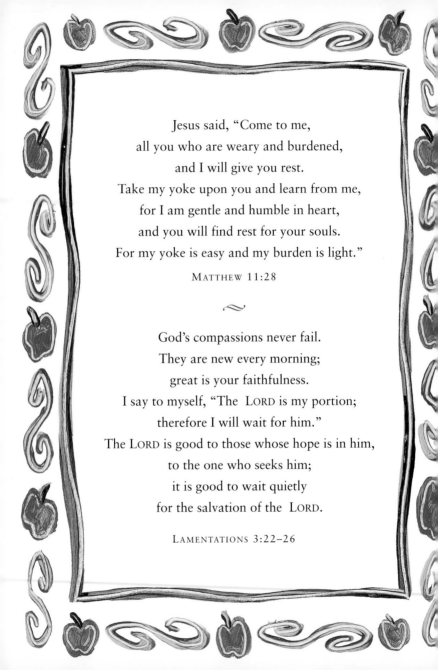

Jesus said, "Come to me,
all you who are weary and burdened,
and I will give you rest.
Take my yoke upon you and learn from me,
for I am gentle and humble in heart,
and you will find rest for your souls.
For my yoke is easy and my burden is light."

MATTHEW 11:28

God's compassions never fail.
They are new every morning;
great is your faithfulness.
I say to myself, "The LORD is my portion;
therefore I will wait for him."
The LORD is good to those whose hope is in him,
to the one who seeks him;
it is good to wait quietly
for the salvation of the LORD.

LAMENTATIONS 3:22–26

*D*o you ever feel as though you have nothing to give? That so many demands are made of you that you've become depleted, empty, exhausted?

I have great news. There is a rest for us—a rest more rejuvenating than a long and leisurely nap, and more soothing to frayed nerves than a Brahms lullaby. This rest reaches into the depths of our souls and claims us from within.

This special promise of rest comes from Jesus' words in Matthew 11:29: "Take my yoke upon you and learn from me ... and you will find rest." Rest for the soul is the most desirable rest. It affects not only our spiritual health but our emotional and physical health as well. The only way to receive this rest is to sit at Christ's feet and hear his word, to take the time to learn more about who he is and what he is like.

DIANE HEAD

$\mathcal{B}$y tenth grade my friends and I had all heard the legend of Mr. Prins, the calculus teacher, and we feared him intensely. From the first day it was only too clear to us that for the next fifteen weeks it would be every nerd for himself.

"Up! Get up!" he barked ferociously. As fast as I could, I scrambled to my feet. I would be his first victim. "Up on your pedestal; we need to see your genius in action, put you on display, Brother Matuszak. Let's hear you sing the squares of twelve through twenty-six to the tune of 'Row, Row, Row Your Boat,'" he commanded. Meekly, monotonously, with hand and brow drenched in ominous sweat I began: "Twelve times twelve is one ..."

"No, no, no," he interrupted, "like you mean it." He proceeded to demonstrate in his best Pavarotti impression. I was terrified beyond the capacity for rational thought as I began my mathematical serenade again.

At this point my peers and I had been told for several years that we were the best and the brightest, the chosen, with the highest potential. Now in my later years I realize that was just undeserved pampering, but at the time we all believed that the rest of life would be as easy as an eighth-grade book report. We were accustomed to teachers being impressed with us. This was the first trial for us, the gauntlet thrown by Mr. Prins. He constantly taunted us up at the blackboard with unsolvable riddles, pushing us to the limit.

Mr. Prins preached one concept above all, a guide for me in every trial I have faced since: mental toughness. He presented the most memorable challenge I faced in my young life. For this I will always be indebted to him. He made me think outside the box of high school mathematics and understand the infinite possibilities and infinite pitfalls all around. He forced us to take the first step towards adulthood when everyone around us became caught up in the last fleeting moments of immaturity.

PETE MATUSZAK

Let us learn together what is good.

JOB 34:4

❧

Be strong in the Lord
and in his mighty power.

EPHESIANS 6:10

❧

Remember your leaders,
who spoke the word of God to you.
Consider the outcome of their way of life
and imitate their faith.

HEBREWS 13:7

❧

Even youths grow tired and weary,
and young men stumble and fall;
but those who hope in the LORD *will renew*
their strength. They will soar on wings like eagles;
they will run and not grow weary,
they will walk and not be faint.

ISAIAH 40:30–31

ost teachers looking back will say they had a horrible first year! But they also will advise that teaching gets easier as each year passes and that they learn at least as much from the experiences as do their students. They are befriended by teaching mentors and learn to ask many and frequent questions everywhere and of everyone. They quit trying to be perfect when they realize that students will learn as much from mistakes as from letter-perfect, planned lessons.

ANN

$\mathcal{A}$t the end of what
had probably been one of the worst
mornings of a truly discouraging week in
the classroom, I dragged into the teachers'
lounge to collapse for my lunch break. I didn't
have much hope that even the high-test, teacher-strength
coffee from the giant lounge percolator would be able
to energize me to return to my classroom when the
bell rang. When I reached the coffee counter, I found a
surprise that just made my day, and I went back to my
room with new hope. There was a red wicker basket full
of cookies and apples. A flowered note card attached to
the handle read: "Dear Teachers: We are praying for you
today! God bless you, Moms in Touch."

PAT MATUSZAK

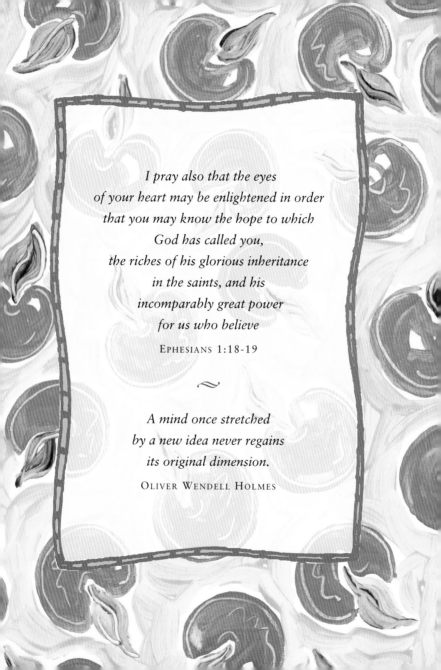

*I pray also that the eyes
of your heart may be enlightened in order
that you may know the hope to which
God has called you,
the riches of his glorious inheritance
in the saints, and his
incomparably great power
for us who believe*

Ephesians 1:18-19

~

*A mind once stretched
by a new idea never regains
its original dimension.*

Oliver Wendell Holmes

*N*ext time you think you hear nothing in response to your prayers, don't assume God isn't listening. He may simply want you to rest in his shadow until he reveals his answer. When you hear a direct no, remind yourself there will always be a better yes. God is for you, and he will work out everything in conformity with the purpose of his will. Everything.

I pray for you and for myself—that we will both grow in our faith. That the times we doubt God will grow fewer and fewer and that the eyes of our hearts will be enlightened. That we may know God's goodness.

KATHY TROCCOLI

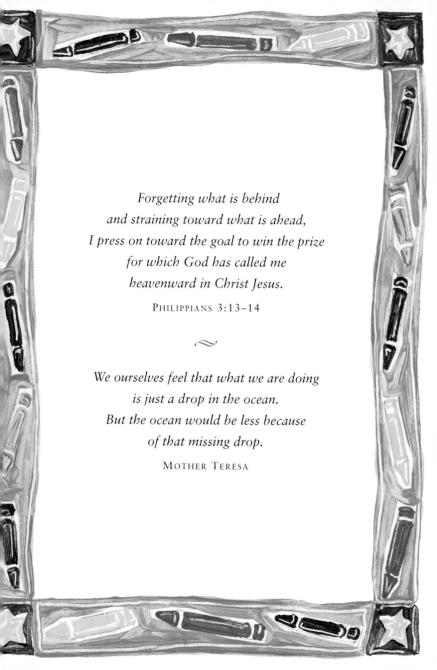

*Forgetting what is behind
and straining toward what is ahead,
I press on toward the goal to win the prize
for which God has called me
heavenward in Christ Jesus.*

PHILIPPIANS 3:13–14

~

*We ourselves feel that what we are doing
is just a drop in the ocean.
But the ocean would be less because
of that missing drop.*

MOTHER TERESA

Thank You God,
from a Teacher's Heart

Thanks, God,
that I had to tell my students
to put their snacks away until break time.
In a world where children are starving,
these little ones have plenty to eat.
And I also thank you for this messy pile
of lost-and-found mittens, hats, and sweaters.
It shows they have plenty of clothes to wear.
Thank you that I goofed up
the wonderful lesson illustration I'd planned.
It means I'm not too old to learn
something new myself. And I also thank you
for the noisy energy of my class at recess.
I'm thankful these kids are
healthy and able to run and play.

PAT MATUSZAK

Let the peace of Christ rule in your hearts,
since as members of one body
you were called to peace.
And be thankful.
Let the word of Christ dwell
in you richly as you teach and
admonish one another with all wisdom,
and as you sing psalms,
hymns and spiritual songs
with gratitude in your hearts to God.
And whatever you do,
whether in word or deed, do it all
in the name of the Lord Jesus,
giving thanks to God the Father through him.

Colossians 3:15–17

*A*ll of his students agreed that Dr. Glenn Fetzer was one of the most kind and understanding college professors we knew. At the same time, his French literature classes, conducted entirely in French, were the most challenging classes we attended. While we appreciated that he had enough respect for our dubious undergrad talents not to dumb down his lectures, we all felt "brain-fried" after class and would just sit and stare at each other in the coffee shop, waiting for our mental hardware to resuscitate.

One day Dr. Fetzer corrected our pronunciation of the term "theorist" which we were pronouncing more like "terrorist" in French. "You don't want to get the two mixed up," he smiled. After class we concluded that he probably suspected some of us were turning out to be literary terrorists, rather than theorists, after reading our essays. Still, for the sake of poetic justice, he was the one we decided to nickname "the literary terrorist."

PAT MATUSZAK

88

She greets a roomful of faces
She's never seen before.
They look at her expectantly
As they file through the door.

There's diversity in her audience.
No two are quite the same.
Each has a different story
To go with the different names.

It's up to her to prepare them
For the steps they'll have to take.
Decisions stand before her,
That she is ready to make.

All her years of training
Have brought her to this place,
With a personal commitment
To every single face.

She walks up to the chalkboard
Then turns to face the masses.
"Good Morning! I'm Mrs. Boyd.
Welcome second grade classes!"

PAM BOYD ALSOVER

*D*evelop a sixth sense about your students. Learn to tell when they are having a bad day, and give them the space they need to cope with it. One piece of advice an assistant principal gave me my first day on the job was, "It is easier to lighten up than to tighten up." So far that has proven true for me. Each class knows on day one what I will tolerate, and everyone gets along a whole lot better because of it. Kids hate surprises.

MRS. B

~

Advice to new teachers:
Don't smile for the first six weeks.

OLD TEACHER SAYING

Teach me, my God and King,
In all things thee to see;
Teach me to be in everything;
All thou wouldst have me be.

In all I think or say, Lord,
May I not offend.
In all I do, be thou the way;
In all be thou the end.

Each task I undertake,
Though weak and mean to me,
If undertaken for thy sake;
Draws strength and worth from thee.

Teach me, then, Lord, to bring,
To all that I may be,
To all I do, my God and King,
A consciousness of thee.

GEORGE HERBERT

$\mathcal{M}$arian Sakalauskas has one of those wise-looking faces that make worried students take comfort. Her brown eyes always seem to be looking right into your soul, and she has just the right smile to let you know she will understand the humor or the seriousness of a situation.

At the high school where she teaches French, Marian is famous for her spontaneity in the classroom and her willingness to miss her lunch hour to fill in for an absent colleague. After school, students often burst into her classroom and confront her with crisis scenarios from different school projects she is coordinating.

She listens carefully to the deluge of words, considers the problem for a moment, then calmly comes up with an acceptable suggestion for each frantic teen. "Don't worry," she smiles. "We'll handle it."

PAT MATUSZAK

If I speak in the tongues of men and of angels, but have not love, I am only a resounding gong or a clanging cymbal. If I have the gift of prophecy and can fathom all mysteries and all knowledge, and if I have a faith that can move mountains, but have not love, I am nothing.

If I give all I possess to the poor and surrender my body to the flames, but have not love, I gain nothing.

Love is patient, love is kind. It does not envy, it does not boast, it is not proud. It is not rude, it is not self-seeking, it is not easily angered, it keeps no record of wrongs. Love does not delight in evil but rejoices with the truth. It always protects, always trusts, always hopes, always perseveres.

Love never fails. But where there are prophecies, they will cease; where there are tongues, they will be stilled; where there is knowledge, it will pass away. For we know in part and we prophesy in part, but when perfection comes, the imperfect disappears.

When I was a child, I talked like a child, I thought like a child, I reasoned like a child. When I became a man, I put childish ways behind me. Now we see but a poor reflection as in a mirror; then we shall see face to face. Now I know in part; then I shall know fully, even as I am fully known.

And now these three remain: faith, hope and love. But the greatest of these is love.

1 CORINTHIANS 13:1–13

*C*hange starts with one person. Any candle we light does make the darkness a little less. Here's to lighting those candles!

I have never given up on people in all of these years. I once learned that I should look for the good in all people. I try to do that. That keeps me optimistic because I usually am able to find at least a shred of goodness in the people I meet!

I only wish that I could eliminate prejudice. I wish people would realize they are more alike than they are different. Bottom line—we are all in this thing called life together; we should work together to make it the best we can and perhaps to leave it in a little better shape than it was.

Here's to remaining positive and to making a difference!

I am a veteran teacher (thirty-two years), and if I can be of any help, I will do what I can! Opening the doors for students is so important!

As for discipline, everyone has his or her own style, but I can tell you what has worked for me, and I have very few discipline problems. I basically treat students the way I would want to be treated. I treat them with respect, and they give it back to me. I am very open with them, too. I tell them that I care about them, and because I care, I work hard to make sure they have skills; however, I also tell them that it is their decision whether or not they are going to be successful. It has worked for me. I guess the big thing is establishing a rapport with your students. They need to know that you are human, too!

Thank You, God, from a Teacher's Heart

Thank you, God, for all the people,
needs, and tasks this day.
Thank you for adventures and misadventures;
May I see the blessings in every one.

Lord, the presence of all
these responsibilities before me Says
you have richly blessed me
with special gifts and graces.
I will do my best to unwrap them all
with a grateful heart.
Amen.

PAT MATUSZAK

SOURCES

Thank you to friends and colleagues who contributed stories to this collection.

Bush, Barbara. *Heart Trouble.*
    Grand Rapids: ZondervanPublishingHouse, 1981.

Fisher, Patricia Ann. *Lord, Don't Let It Rain at Recess.*
    Grand Rapids: ZondervanPublishingHouse, 1988.

Fisher, Patricia Ann. *The Gospel According to First Grade.*
    Grand Rapids: ZondervanPublishingHouse, 1995.

Graham, Billy. *Just As I Am.*
    HarperCollins/ZondervanPublishingHouse, 1997.

Head, Diane. *Come to the Waters.*
    Grand Rapids: ZondervanPublishingHouse, 1985.

Matuszak, Pat. *Teacher Stories.* published at
    http://memberpage.women.com/spirituality/booklink/teacher.html

Swindoll, Luci. *Women's Devotional Bible.*
    Grand Rapids: ZondervanPublishingHouse, 1990.

Thomas, Cal. *Blinded By Might.*
    Grand Rapids: ZondervanPublishingHouse, 1998.

Tucker, Ruth. *Women's Devotional Bible.*
    Grand Rapids: ZondervanPublishingHouse, 1990.

Rinker, Rosalind. *Women's Devotional Bible.*
    Grand Rapids: ZondervanPublishingHouse, 1990.

MacDonald, Hope. *Women's Devotional Bible.*
    Grand Rapids: ZondervanPublishingHouse, 1990.

Troccoli, Kathy. *My Life Is in Your Hands.*
    Grand Rapids: ZondervanPublishingHouse, 1997.

Walsh, Sheila. *Faith, Hope, Love: Scripture and Lyrics to
    Bring Joy to Your Heart and Peace to Your Soul.*
    Grand Rapids: ZondervanPublishingHouse, 1998.